Discovering the Old Testament

by
Fr Adrian Graffy

*All booklets are published thanks to the
generous support of the members of the
Catholic Truth Society*

CATHOLIC TRUTH SOCIETY
PUBLISHERS TO THE HOLY SEE

Contents

ISBN 978 1 86082 929 1

The Books of the Old Testament

The Pentateuch	*The Wisdom Books*
Genesis	Proverbs
Exodus	Job
Leviticus	Ecclesiastes (Qoheleth)
Numbers	Ecclesiasticus (Sirach)*
Deuteronomy	Wisdom*
	Psalms
	Song of Songs
The Historical Books	*The Prophets*
Deuteronomistic History:	*Major Prophets:*
Joshua	Isaiah
Judges	Jeremiah
1 Samuel	Lamentations
2 Samuel	Baruch*
1 Kings	Ezekiel
2 Kings	Daniel
Chronicler's History:	*Minor Prophets:*
1 Chronicles	Hosea
2 Chronicles	Joel
Ezra	Amos
Nehemiah	Obadiah
1 Maccabees*	Jonah
2 Maccabees*	Micah
Ruth	Nahum
Tobit*	Habakkuk
Judith*	Zephaniah
Esther	Haggai
	Zechariah
	Malachi

* denotes deutero-canonical books.

Encouragement from Pope Francis

In his exhortation *Evangelii Gaudium* ('The Joy of the Gospel') Pope Francis reminds us that all Christians are called to spread the good news of Jesus Christ. We are all invited to evangelise. "There is a kind of preaching which falls to each of us as a daily responsibility. It has to do with bringing the Gospel to people we meet, whether they be our neighbours or complete strangers."

Pope Francis explains that all evangelisation is based on the word of God "listened to, meditated upon, lived, celebrated and witnessed to". The Scriptures of the Old and New Testaments are the source for evangelisation. The word of God, listened to and celebrated above all in the Eucharist, enables us to offer witness in our daily lives. "The preaching of the word, living and effective, prepares for the reception of the Sacrament, and in the Sacrament that word attains its maximum efficacy."

The study of the word of God must be "a door opened to every believer". Enriched by the word of God we can both live our faith and bear witness to it. This study of the Bible must be accompanied by "prayerful individual and communal reading".

Some final words from Pope Francis: "The best incentive for sharing the Gospel comes from contemplating it with love, lingering over its pages and reading it with the heart. If we approach it in this way, its beauty will amaze and constantly excite us."

Introduction

Every piece of Scripture is inspired by God, and useful for teaching, for correcting error, for guidance and for training in righteousness.

These words from the Second Letter to Timothy (3:16) are a constant challenge to Christians. To receive the teaching and guidance the Scriptures convey is not always easy. This is particularly true of the Old Testament. How can these Scriptures be considered useful today? Are they not far too much a product of ancient times? Are they not superseded for Christians by the New Testament?

This booklet offers a way forward to a deeper understanding of the Old Testament. It can be used either by individuals or by groups. As you go through the booklet, it will be helpful to read the individual chapters of the Old Testament which are mentioned. The biblical verses quoted at the beginning of each section may be tracked down in the Bible and the surrounding text explored. You may wish to read the sections in a different order. Begin with whichever part of the Old Testament attracts your interest. You may like to re-read the section on a particular book when that book is being read in the liturgy or being used in your prayer group or bible group.

After some introductory questions this booklet will look first at the books of the Pentateuch. We will then consider the books known as "historical". The major and minor prophets will be viewed next. Finally we will survey the psalms, the books known as "wisdom literature", and the latest books of the Old Testament.

The Old Testament and the Church

The relationship of the Church to the Old Testament has sometimes been a difficult one. There have been some who have considered that the Old Testament ought to be rejected. The heretic Marcion in the middle of the second century AD taught that the Gospel of Luke and the letters of Paul were all a Christian needed. And yet, from the New Testament itself, with its abundant use of the Old Testament, it is obvious that these Scriptures of Judaism, the Scriptures which Jesus knew, were always important for his followers.

The twentieth century of Christianity saw a remarkable deepening of appreciation of the Bible among Catholics. They have learned to treasure the whole of the Bible, both Old and New Testaments, and they have begun to value the Old Testament not only as preparation for the coming of Jesus but also in its own right.

The encyclical *Divino Afflante Spiritu* issued in 1943 by Pope Pius XII encouraged students of the Bible in the

Catholic Church to adopt without fear modern methods of study developed by other Christians. They should be more aware of the historical situations in which the different parts of the Old Testament were produced. Readers of the Old Testament should appreciate that this literature was first written in Hebrew, Aramaic and Greek, and that it was handed down in various translations through the centuries. Most importantly, they should recognise what are known as "literary genres", the different types of writing present in the Scriptures. A piece of prophetic speech is different from a psalm. A theological story should not be treated as a piece of history. They should appreciate the original sense of a text before exploring later interpretations of the same text of Scripture.

In the wake of *Divino Afflante Spiritu*, Catholic scholars made increasingly significant contributions to the interpretation of the Bible. The Second Vatican Council promulgated in 1965 the "Dogmatic Constitution on Divine Revelation", usually known as *Dei Verbum* (Word of God) from its first two Latin words. It remains in our day the fundamental guidance of the Church for the interpretation of the Bible. *Dei Verbum* dedicates the whole of its fourth chapter to the Old Testament.

For Christians the Old Testament prepares for Christ. Christians see in it a developing hope and a developing understanding which reaches fulfilment in the coming of Jesus Christ. As St Augustine of Hippo puts it, "the Old Testament becomes clear in the New, and the New Testament lies hidden in the Old." This close relationship between the two testaments is a major theme of the Council document. But the document also stresses the value of the Old Testament in itself. It has precious and sublime teaching to impart about God and about the human condition. It provides wise counsel about life's problems. It contains a limitless source of prayer, both in the Psalms and in many other books.

Dei Verbum remains the fundamental guidance for Catholics today in all matters concerning Scripture. The teaching of *Dei Verbum* is summarised in the Catechism of the Catholic Church. Another major document on the Bible has been the fruit of the 2008 world Synod of Bishops on 'The Word of God in the Life and Mission of the Church'. Called by Pope Benedict XVI, the synod considered the place of the Bible in the Catholic Church in great detail. Taking into consideration the deliberations of the bishops and adding his own insights, Pope Benedict prepared his 'post-synodal apostolic exhortation', which is entitled *Verbum Domini*. After the introduction there are three principal parts: 'the Word of God', 'the Word in the Church' and 'the Word to the World'. *Verbum Domini* is a magnificent survey of the role that the Bible plays in the life of faith. Pope Benedict, together with the bishops of the world, expressed the hope for "a new season of greater love for sacred Scripture".

Problems and pitfalls

It is no exaggeration to say that certain texts in the Old Testament can cause considerable confusion and bewilderment for Christian readers. When Christians read that God gives the command that Israel should slaughter its enemies, they are understandably troubled. When God is stated to have decreed the death of David's new-born son as a punishment for David's sin, they have questions concerning God's justice. When a psalmist delivers harsh curses against personal enemies or the enemies of the nation, they feel uncomfortable. In all these cases it is essential to recall that the Bible, both in the Old Testament and in the New, reflects a journey of discovery, a journey towards understanding. The Spirit of God guides the people of God towards the complete truth. But it is made clear repeatedly in the teaching of the Church that the Scriptures give us the Word of God in human language. God's words are channelled through human words. Human limitations, human prejudices and human mistakes are evident in the scriptural texts. *Dei Verbum* affirms that the Old Testament contains things which are "imperfect and time-conditioned" (*Dei Verbum*, 15). Particular understandings of God's ways and God's law are put aside as time passes to be replaced by new insights given by the Spirit of God. The Council is at the same time very clear that in matters concerning our salvation the Scriptures do not contain error (*Dei Verbum*, 11).

Another major problem has already been hinted at. To understand a biblical text correctly it is necessary to be aware of the "literary genre", the kind of writing used by the writer in a particular text. The first chapter of Genesis is not intended as a historical account of God's work of creation, but is an inspired poetic narrative in praise of the creator. The apocalyptic visions of Daniel are fundamentally expressions of future hope written for their own times, and should not be treated as precise forecasts of dates and future events which readers may apply to their own age. By showing respect for the intention of the writer we can avoid the danger of fundamentalism, and its tendency to attribute historical value to texts in an inappropriate way.

Which Bible should I read?

A question people often ask when deciding to read the Bible more regularly is "which Bible should I read?" A rich and somewhat bewildering variety of translations and editions of the Bible can be found in religious bookshops these days. To aid understanding it is clearly best to choose a modern translation. The "King James Bible", also known as the "Authorized Version", contains some of the most beautiful English ever written and is rightly treasured as a work of literature. It is, however, not easy for modern readers to understand, and, being written in the early seventeenth century, lacks the benefit of later progress in understanding the Scriptures. Catholic translations like the "Douai Bible" and the "Knox Bible" are also dated, and these Bibles also suffer from the fact that they were translated not from the original languages but from the Latin Vulgate translation, the official Latin translation used by the Church since the fifth century.

To assist understanding the Catholic Church encourages the production of annotated Bibles. The annotated "Jerusalem Bible" or its successor the "New Jerusalem Bible" not only provide useful information in the notes whether you read the study edition or the reader's edition, but also neatly divide the text into manageable sections rather than presenting it without breaks. Each section is given a title so that the reader is assisted in grasping the meaning. The annotated "Revised Standard Version" and "New Revised Standard Version" have similar strengths. These are the Bibles which would be best suited to Catholic readers today. Several different editions of each translation are often available. Examine them and choose the Bible which seems most attractive.

Mention should also be made of the "New International Version", a widely-available Bible which reflects more conservative positions on interpretation. The "New English Bible" and its successor the "Revised English Bible" provide translations in modern English style and take less conservative positions. The "Good News Bible" seems a very attractive translation, but it often paraphrases a translation to make the text more intelligible and will not be the best version for anyone wanting to get close to the original expressions of the biblical writers. Whatever Bible you buy, it is most important to make sure that it contains the "deutero-canonical" books (see the list at the front of this book), which are described as "the apocrypha" in non-Catholic Bibles. More will be said about these seven books in the next section.

The canon of the Old Testament

Anyone wishing to become familiar with the Old Testament must first be aware of the "canon". This is the name given to the list of books recognised by the Church as inspired Scripture. The canon of the Old Testament has its origins of course in Judaism, but it seems to have been only in the first century AD that Jewish leaders decided on a fixed canon. The books of the developing Hebrew Bible were known as the *torah* (which means "instruction" or "teaching"), the *nebiim* ("prophets"), and the *ketubim* ("writings"). We find a reference to the Old Testament as having three parts in the Gospel of Luke 24:44, which speaks of "the law of Moses, the prophets and the psalms".

The acceptance of the canon of the Old Testament was however more complex than a simple adoption by Christians of the Jewish canon. In the final centuries before Christ the Jews at Alexandria in Egypt had produced a translation of the Hebrew Scriptures. It was in Greek, the language established throughout the eastern Mediterranean as an international language due to the conquests of Alexander the Great. In Egypt a larger collection of books emerged. The seven extra books found in the Greek canon are known in Catholic circles as "deutero-canonicals", and more generally as "apocrypha". They are the books of 1 and 2 Maccabees, the books of Baruch, Tobit, Judith, Sirach (Ecclesiasticus), and Wisdom. This Greek Bible came to be known as the Septuagint, due to the legend of the seventy-two translators who produced it. It was this longer canon which Christians generally adopted. At the time of the Reformation, some Christians expressed once again ancient doubts about the inspired nature of the extra books and promoted the shorter canon of the Old Testament. Catholic teaching is quite clear that the extra books are inspired Scripture.

As well as adopting the extra books found in the Greek canon Christians also adopted a different division of the Scriptures. It is customary for us to consider the Old Testament as consisting of the Pentateuch, the Historical books, the Prophets, and the Wisdom books. See the list in this booklet (page 3), for details, or consult the table of contents given in your own Bible. This clustering of books suggests similarities between them. Books of historical narrative will have common features. A prophetic book can be expected to contain speeches of a prophet. Within each major division of the Old Testament there may be found collections, such as the books known as the "deuteronomistic history", and the collection of twelve books known as the "minor prophets". Such sections will have had their own process of composition and compilation before being incorporated into the Bible.

Scripture and Prayer

Anyone hearing or reading the Gospels or other books of the New Testament soon realises the need to read the Old Testament too. To neglect the Old Testament in one's reading of Scripture is to deprive oneself of one of the two lungs of Scripture.

Catholics are accustomed to hearing pieces of the Old Testament from the lectionary at Mass, both on Sundays and on weekdays. Those who are familiar with the Liturgy of the Hours (the Divine Office or breviary) will have further exposure to the Old Testament. How can we assist our understanding of these readings and prayers? A quiet preparatory reading of the Scriptures before Mass can lay the foundations for a more fruitful listening. One may well wish to return to these Scriptures again later. It is a good idea to read the liturgical texts from the Bible so that we can be aware of the context of the readings and take advantage of the explanatory notes.

Putting aside regular time to read the Scriptures in a quiet and calm fashion leads to an ability to pray the Scriptures.

This meditative, peaceful reading has been practised for centuries in the Church and is known as *lectio divina* or "divine reading". Whether practised in relation to the liturgical readings or separately it is a most fruitful way of reading the Scriptures. In *lectio divina* reading and prayer meet. Each person will learn how to use the Scriptures in prayer by a regular commitment to this reading.

During the twentieth century the Catholic Church reached a deeper appreciation of the gift of the Scriptures, and encouraged more than ever before the use of the Bible by all the faithful. This is a challenge for us in the third millennium of Christian faith. It is true that people need assistance to be able to profit from their reading. It helps to know certain facts, even certain historical dates. With a minimum of introductory information the reader can make a start. In the end the essential element to bring to one's reading is a listening heart, a heart wishing to understand, a heart that is open to prayer. When he became king, Solomon was allowed a request from God. He asked for a "listening heart". You can read the story in 1 Kings, chapter 3. This gift of a "listening heart" is the gift of God which all of us who read the Scriptures also seek.

The Pentateuch

The book of Genesis

In the beginning God created
the heavens and the earth.

(Genesis 1:1)

It is well known that the word "Pentateuch" means "five
volumes". The books of Genesis, Exodus, Leviticus,
Numbers and Deuteronomy are traditionally referred to as
the books of the "Law". The Hebrew word *torah*, used in
Judaism to refer to these five books, is more accurately
translated as "teaching" or "instruction".

The first of these books, the book of Genesis, has had
an enormous impact on Jewish and Christian believers and
on the history of ideas. It is best regarded as composed
of two parts: the first eleven chapters are concerned with
beginnings, and with providing answers to the fundamental
questions people ask, while Genesis 12-50 gives us the
stories of the ancient ancestors of the people of Israel, the
traditions concerning Abraham, Isaac and Jacob and their
descendants.

The stories of creation and the garden of Eden in the
first three chapters of Genesis may well be the best known

parts of the Old Testament. It is crucial when dealing with these chapters to identify the type of writing represented here. These chapters do not provide us with historical accounts. A familiarity with the stories from other civilizations concerning the creation and the flood confirm that what we have here are traditional tales incorporating early Hebrew beliefs about God, human beings, the world, and the presence of good and evil. Creation stories and flood stories from ancient times are of a similar type, though they do not contain the insights of the ancient Hebrews concerning God and human beings.

Genesis, chapter 1, shows God creating an ordered universe. All is good, and man and woman are created in the image of God to be the custodians of the creation. God is presented as resting after six days of work. The six-day creation pattern authorises and sanctifies the sabbath rest for all who work. A second creation tale in Genesis chapter 2 focuses on the creation of the man and his need for companionship. The man relates to the woman and is overjoyed by her creation. This second creation tale portrays God, given the ancient name of Yahweh, in more human terms, to show that God is deeply involved with human beings. God moulds the body of the man and breathes life into his nostrils. The writers of these tales struggle to express the mystery of the creator God, one by stressing God's transcendent greatness and the other by emphasising God's caring involvement.

Genesis, chapter 3, is the story of the disobedience of the man and the woman and their consequent expulsion from God's garden, known traditionally as the "garden of Eden". The story grapples with the entry of sin into the world and the pain and suffering which are considered its results. The instigator of evil is the serpent. The question of why God allows evil to enter the world and where it comes from is not raised. Due to their sin the man and woman are expelled from the garden and lose the closeness of God.

These opening chapters of Genesis present the reality of the human situation and are as valid now as when they were composed. Human beings are aware of God's goodness but also of their distance from God due to evil. The story of Noah sees the flood as a consequence of the increasing presence of evil in the world. God's good creation has been corrupted, and human beings have colluded with evil. But just as God did not abandon Adam and Eve, nor does he abandon Noah and his family. The story of a God who does not cease to care is the continuing story of the Bible.

The second part of the book of Genesis in chapters 12-50 brings us the ancient stories of the first ancestors of the Jewish people. Abraham, Isaac and Jacob, and their wives, Sarah, Rebekah and Rachel, are the people through whom God is seen as faithfully fulfilling a promise of solidarity. Abraham receives a promise of fertile land and numerous children and, as the book progresses, these promises are fulfilled. The gift of a son to Abraham by Sarah is finally received only to be put at risk momentarily when Abraham considers he should sacrifice Isaac. God reassures him that no harm should be done to the boy. Abraham remains faithful and his faith is rewarded. Isaac and Jacob too are recipients of God's promise. The story of Jacob has similar tensions. Through adversity and prosperity and not a little cunning Jacob becomes the revered father of the twelve tribes. His God-given name is Israel, meaning to wrestle with God. The twelve tribes are his descendants.

The fulfilment of the promise is once again at risk in the final chapters of the book of Genesis, chapters 37 to 50, which contain the story of Joseph. With this story the land given by God is lost. But God uses the evil suffered by Joseph at his brothers' hands to good purpose. The exiled Joseph rises to a position of power in Egypt and, when famine drives Jacob's clan south to Egypt, it is Joseph who becomes the instrument of the continuing protection of God and provides food and a livelihood for them.

The story of Moses

There has never arisen in Israel another prophet like Moses, the one whom the Lord knew face to face.

(*Deuteronomy 34:10*)

A major focus for anyone who reads the Pentateuch must be the figure of Moses, who dominates the remaining four books of the Pentateuch. Moses is both liberator and law-giver. Much of the Pentateuch records the laws of the covenant, laws attributed to Moses and understood as the detailed spelling out of what God requires of the people. The book of Exodus begins with a description of the serious situation of the Hebrews in Egypt under a new pharaoh, who did not know Joseph. The descendants of Jacob work as slaves. A decree of genocide, ordering that all Hebrew males be slaughtered at birth makes matters worse.

The God who remained faithful to the ancestors is faithful to the Hebrew people now oppressed in Egypt. Moses has an extraordinary experience of God on the holy mountain known as Sinai, or Horeb, narrated in Exodus, chapter 3. Moses is commanded to speak to the people of God's decision to liberate the nation. The story tells of Moses' visits to the pharaoh with his brother Aaron and of ten plagues inflicted by God on the Egyptians. The book of Exodus contains a most dramatic story of the people's liberation in the account of the crossing of the sea, a story developed to extraordinary proportions in biblical tradition. This theological epic makes clear that God will not allow the people to live in slavery. The God of the people of Israel is a God who wants people to live in freedom.

At this point Exodus, chapter 12, gives instructions on how the liberation was to be celebrated in the yearly festival of Passover. The Jewish Passover, the festival of a freed people, would be used as the basis for the supper Jesus celebrated and told his disciples to celebrate as a festival of the freedom Jesus would win for all.

The liberated people travels to Sinai, the place where Moses met God, the place of God's covenant. Here the relationship of God and the people of Israel is forged. The story of the presence of the people at God's mountain is suitably dramatic too, with thunder and lightning, earthquake and cloud. All this is a prelude to the giving of the laws of the covenant and the solemn sealing of a covenant between God and the people. The covenant is ratified by the sprinkling of blood on the people in Exodus, chapter 24. The Pentateuch will have the people remain at Sinai throughout the rest of the book of Exodus, throughout the whole of the book Leviticus and until well into the book of Numbers, as it lists the laws of the covenant, laws developed over centuries, many of them after the time of Moses.

For Christian believers much of the legislation found in the Pentateuch must be considered outdated. But the books of Exodus, Leviticus and Deuteronomy do contain considerable material which remains of relevance to Christians today. This is true above all of the legislation concerning social life. Care for the poor, the orphans and the widows above all, sensitivity to immigrants and emancipation of slaves are features of this legislation. The social awareness seen here will reappear in the prophets of

Israel, in the New Testament and in the social teaching of the Church. A liberating God also desires people to live in liberty, free from constraints and free from want. The seeds of the social teaching of the Catholic Church are found in the Pentateuch and in the prophets of the Old Testament.

At the end of the Pentateuch in Deuteronomy, chapter 34, we find the story of Moses' death on Mount Nebo, on the borders of the land promised by God. The account of his death provides a solemn conclusion to the five books of the Pentateuch.

The Historical Books

Joshua and the Judges

Arise now and cross this Jordan, you and this whole people, and enter the land which I am giving to them, to the children of Israel.

(Joshua 1:2)

After the Pentateuch we come to a group of books known in Christian circles as the "historical books". Our survey of the Pentateuch has already shown that these stories contain a good deal of teaching about God and God's dealing with the people. As we reach the book of Joshua we are aware of what might be called a "theological history". The stories in these books carry with them a particular understanding of God. The book of Joshua is the first of a set of historical books known by scholars as the "deuteronomistic history" due to their use of the basic theological ideas of the book of Deuteronomy, above all the idea that the course of history is largely determined by the good and evil people do. The books of Joshua, Judges, 1 and 2 Samuel, and 1 and 2 Kings tell of the re-entry of the people into the ancient land of Canaan, and their remaining there until the deportation to Babylon at the beginning of the sixth century BC.

The book of Joshua contains the classic description of Joshua's conquest of the land of Canaan, of which the most celebrated part is surely the fall of the walls of Jericho in chapter 6. Archaeological exploration has in some cases raised questions about the historical accuracy of these tales. What we read here are stories of a warrior God, who achieves the conquest of the land by extraordinary interventions. These tales celebrate God's gift of the land despite opposition and the fulfilment of God's ancient promise. In chapter 10 the story tells of the standing still of the sun so that the Hebrews can slaughter their enemies. The text has no scientific validity, and it contains a portrayal of God as desiring annihilation of the Gibeonites which later biblical tradition would challenge. The God of a chosen people is gradually understood to be the creator and protector of all nations, but such a notion is not in the mind of this writer. It takes time for the people to understand the attitude of God to foreign nations.

While the book of Joshua describes a complete conquest by Joshua and his followers, the book of Judges suggests that things were not so simple. This book uses a stereotyped sequence of events to recount the deeds of military leaders of Israel. Israel's infidelity and worship of pagan gods bring about oppression of Israel by their neighbours. A military leader, known as a "judge", is raised up by God to liberate the people, who after a period of compliance once again turn to other gods. The book of

Judges uses the idea that disobedience brings punishment to explain the course of Israel's history.

The book of Judges contains the stories of Deborah, of Gideon, of Jephthah and of Samson. Jephthah's killing of his daughter in fidelity to a vow is clearly an example of dangerous and outdated morality. The portrayal of Samson shows a primitive conception of how God's spirit works in an individual. The books of Joshua and Judges provide the clearest examples in the Old Testament of outdated ideas about God and about morality. As the tradition develops in the Old and New Testaments these inadequate understandings are replaced. Human life cannot be offered in ritual sacrifice to God. The sufferings of nations and individuals require deeper reflection.

The book of Ruth can be mentioned here since it is set in the period of the judges. It narrates how Ruth, a Moabite woman who had married an Israelite in the land of Moab, is left a childless widow on his death and shows fidelity to her Israelite mother-in-law, Naomi. Ruth finds a new husband when she travels back to the land of Israel with Naomi. The quiet strength and goodness of Ruth, who becomes ancestress to king David, provides a more enduring insight into the working of God's spirit in the life of the individual.

David and Solomon

Your house and your kingdom will remain firm for ever
before me, and your throne will be secure for ever.

(2 Samuel 7:16)

The book of Judges reported a couple of attempts,
in the stories of Gideon and Abimelech, to establish a
monarchy in Israel as a means of unifying the nation in
face of foreign threats. As the first book of Samuel begins
there is clearly a struggle between those who wish to
establish kingship as the way of governing the nation and
those who consider this would be an insult to the God
who alone is king. Despite misgivings Saul is anointed
as the first king of the tribes of Israel. His career is a
disaster, for he lacks support from the prophet Samuel,
who in the traditional stories seems too ready to find fault
with Saul. Saul's faults, which are due to inexperience
and lack of wisdom, are punished by Samuel with his
announcement of God's rejection. It is the rise of the
young hero David, however, which fatally undermines
Saul. Saul dies in battle with the Philistines as the first
book of Samuel ends.

While there was a clear reluctance to accept Saul as
king, David is made king with the wholehearted support of
the tribe of Judah and the other tribes of Israel. He captures
the ancient city of Jerusalem and makes it his capital. In

the second book of Samuel a new theology emerges in which the king is seen as God's regent, proclaimed "son of God", through whom God renews a covenant commitment with the people. The seventh chapter of 2 Samuel is rightly considered a major step forward in the Old Testament. The idea of the constant fidelity of God to the king found in this chapter will eventually give rise to hopes of a future ideal messiah, or "anointed one", provided by God. The prophets and the psalmists will express such hopes, which will be crucial in Christian understanding of Jesus.

The portrayal of David in the second book of Samuel shows his special rapport with God. But David's limitations are also honestly portrayed. This is evident more than anywhere else in his adultery with Bathsheba and arranged murder of her husband Uriah the Hittite. The subsequent troubles in David's family are considered to be caused by his own sins. The revolt of David's son Absalom against his father and David's flight from Jerusalem are the lowest point of his reign, but David eventually returns. Finally David dies and Solomon, his second son by Bathsheba, takes the throne amid considerable intrigue.

Solomon is recorded as the most prosperous and wise of kings in the early chapters of the first book of Kings. He is reputed to be a man of great learning and wisdom. He consolidates his kingdom by eliminating opposition and by marrying into the families of foreign rulers. Among his numerous wives is the daughter of the pharaoh.

He implements the plans for building a temple to God in Jerusalem. Several chapters are dedicated to this enterprise.

Yet Solomon too has his faults. He enslaves both foreigners and native Israelites for the work of fortifying cities and building the temple and his own palace. The writer of 1 Kings records that his many pagan wives led him to worship other gods and that for this reason the unity of the tribe of Judah with the other tribes of Israel would come to an end at Solomon's death. The collapse of the union at the death of Solomon is interpreted as due to Solomon's faults. Perhaps it is truer to say that it was due to his poor treatment of the tribes of Israel in imposition of excessive taxes and hard labour. The Solomon cherished by later tradition will nevertheless be a man of wisdom, to whom some of the books known as "wisdom writings" are attributed.

The kingdoms of Judah and Israel

He burned down the house of the Lord, and the house of the king, and all the houses of Jerusalem, every great house he burned down.

(*2 Kings 25:9*)

The united kingdom splits apart at the death of Solomon. The kingdom of Judah in the south will have descendants of David as its rulers. The tribes of Israel in the north are initially led by Jeroboam I. The political split is accompanied by a religious division. Temple worship continues in Solomon's temple in Jerusalem. Jeroboam, on the other hand, establishes two centres of worship in the northern kingdom at the ancient sites of Bethel and Dan. The writer of 1 Kings denounces this development. Indeed, Jeroboam and his successors on the throne of Israel are judged in a most negative light. From 1 Kings, chapter 12, the books of Kings record parallel histories of the kings of the south and the kings of the north.

As the first book of Kings continues, the focus moves from kings to prophets as the stories of the great Elijah are set in writing. Prophecy begins in early times but comes to its flowering in the period of the kings of Israel and Judah. Elijah's task is to confront Ahab, king of Israel, for he has colluded with the policy of his pagan wife Jezebel to establish worship of the pagan gods and outlaw the worship of Yahweh. Elijah's very name, which means "my God is Yahweh", testifies to his mission. Elijah challenges the pagan prophets to a contest on Mount Carmel in 1 Kings chapter 18. Despite their pleadings, rantings and ravings, these prophets are unable to call down a response from their gods. Elijah brings down fire from heaven to consume the offering he has prepared. The same Elijah journeys to Horeb, the mountain also called Sinai, and there encounters Yahweh, not in the wind, nor in the earthquake, nor in the fire, but in a still, small voice (1 Kings chapter 19). The God of power is also a God of peace. A final important dimension of Elijah's ministry is seen in his confrontation with Ahab who usurps Naboth's vineyard after Jezebel has had Naboth killed. Elijah, recalling the laws of the covenant and preparing for many later prophets, proclaims God's command of social justice and respect for the rights of the less powerful. As the second book of Kings begins, we reach the end of the Elijah stories. Elijah is taken to God in a fiery chariot. His disciple Elisha inherits his mantle.

The remaining chapters of the second book of Kings focus once again on political events. The empire of Assyria takes control of the region in the middle of the eighth century BC. Israel and then Judah become vassals to the Assyrians. By 721 BC, the northern kingdom is overrun by the Assyrian armies as punishment for joining an anti-Assyrian alliance. The northern kingdom comes to an end. Judah manages to survive despite the revolt of the good king Hezekiah. This is the time of the great prophet Isaiah, of whom more will be said later. When power passes from Assyria to Babylon in the last years of the seventh century BC Judah is forced to submit to Nebuchadnezzar. Amid an extraordinarily complex series of events, with power shifting from one empire to another, the prophet Jeremiah preaches acceptance of foreign domination. The second book of Kings ends with the revolts of Judah against Babylon, deportations of the people to Babylon in successive stages, and the destruction of the city of Jerusalem and its temple.

The deuteronomistic history began with the entry into the land under Joshua. It ends with the deportation from the land. The troubles suffered by the people are understood as due to their infidelity, their turning to false gods and pagan overlords. The final trauma of loss of land and loss of temple will bring about a profound re-thinking of their faith and life.

We should take note at this point of other groups of books known as "historical". The Chronicler's history, comprising 1 and 2 Chronicles and the books of Ezra and Nehemiah, is foremost among these. The first book of Chronicles begins with ancient genealogical lists of names. It is when the history reaches king David that we can see how different it is from the deuteronomistic history. David and Solomon are simply men of God for the chronicler. Negative deeds reported in the books of Samuel and Kings are eliminated here. Only good things can be reported of David for he is the one who planned the building of the temple. Only good deeds can be reported of Solomon for he built the temple and presided at its opening. The Chronicler gives only the briefest mention of the break-up of the two kingdoms and does not provide a history of the northern kingdom of Israel. This history emphasises the deeds of good kings who are remembered as strengthening the people of God as a worshipping community. The trend continues in the books of Ezra and Nehemiah, which are our major source for traditions about the rebuilding of the temple and the city of Jerusalem after the return from Babylon.

Christian tradition has included other books as "historical". Due to their late date the two books of Maccabees and the stories of Tobit, Judith and Esther are better considered in the final sections of this booklet.

The Prophets

Prophets of the eighth century

Here I am. Send me.

(Isaiah 6:8)

The history of the kings of Israel and Judah runs parallel to
the history of the prophets. It is time now to consider the
books attributed to the prophets, both the major prophets
(Isaiah, Jeremiah and Ezekiel), and the twelve minor
prophets. We will consider them as far as possible in
chronological order rather than in the order in which they
appear in the Bible, so that their place in history can assist
an understanding of their message. The books of Baruch
and Daniel will be treated later due to their late date.

A prophet is fundamentally a communicator of God's
word. The prophet addresses first and foremost the people
of his own time, to challenge and reprove, to encourage and
console. The role of the prophet is to speak to individuals
and to groups. The words of prophets were remembered and
finally recorded. The books of the prophets contain only
rare references to this process of recording their teachings.
It is known that Jeremiah had a scribe called Baruch,

but usually we have little or no information concerning how a prophet's words came to be written down.

The earliest of those prophets to whom books of the Old Testament are attributed are Amos and Hosea. Both preached in the northern kingdom of Israel in the last years of that kingdom's existence. Amos, a shepherd of Judah driven by an irresistible call of God, goes to the kingdom of Israel to preach against social injustice. With the coming of the monarchy social divisions have arisen. People fall into debt and into slavery. Amos challenges the ill-treatment of the poor, who by the laws of the covenant should receive special consideration. He reproves the rich for the extravagance of their lifestyle. While the poor are not assisted, people delight in elaborate liturgies with chanting and strumming of harps. It seems that the patience of God is exhausted and that there is no future for the people.

The prophet Hosea complements the vigorous message of Amos by describing a loving God, who is torn between condemnation of Israel and forgiveness. Hosea uses his own personal experience of loving an unfaithful wife to express the dilemma of God. The prophet speaks of Israel's religious infidelity in worshipping the local gods in addition to the God of Israel. He speaks of their political infidelity in seeking protection from pagan empires rather than trusting in God. He uses quite violent language to express God's disappointed love, but God is also determined not to give way to fierce anger. In the final chapter of the book Hosea speaks tenderly of God's faithful love of Israel. The constancy of God continues despite the infidelity of the people. Hosea makes a major contribution to the understanding of God in the Old Testament by drawing the parallel between his own marital experience and God's love for Israel.

Contemporaries of Hosea in the kingdom of Judah are the great prophet Isaiah and the minor prophet Micah. The book of the prophet Isaiah is one of the longest books of the entire Bible, but only thirty-nine of its sixty-six chapters are concerned with the Isaiah who was prophet in Jerusalem in the second half of the eighth century BC. Further material from later prophets has been added to the book in the course of its compilation over centuries.

We read of the call of the prophet Isaiah in chapter 6 of the book. Isaiah is overcome with awe when he receives a vision of God in the temple. Aware that God is sending him to preach, Isaiah is deeply conscious of his own unworthiness. The prophet's lips are symbolically purified and he is made aware of the difficulties of his task. Isaiah calls on his contemporaries to have faith, to trust in God and in the promises made to David. In the days of Isaiah the kingdom of Judah comes under threat both from neighbouring kingdoms and from the Assyrian empire. Isaiah constantly encourages the kings of Judah to trust.

Isaiah is revered by Christians as the prophet of the messiah. This feature of his preaching is closely related to trusting in God's promise to David. The God who, in Isaiah's view, guarantees the safety of the nation will continue to provide for the people through the sons of David, kings of David's line. The anointed one, the messiah, is the name given to the ideal king for whose coming the people hope. God's promise of solidarity is realised in the continuing davidic line. In chapter 7 Isaiah speaks of the birth of a child as a sign for the king. The child will be called Immanuel, which means "God is with us". Two magnificent poems in chapter 9 and chapter 11 look forward to the coming of the ideal king. The birth of a new king will bring light to a darkened land. He will be a man of wisdom and strength. His kingdom will bring true justice and peace. This king will receive the spirit and all the spirit's gifts. It is no surprise that the poems of Isaiah fuelled hopes of an ideal future king, and are considered fulfilled by Christians in the coming of Jesus.

Isaiah also followed the tradition of Elijah and Amos and spoke out for social justice. God's solidarity with the davidic king was a solidarity with the whole nation. God's challenge to king and people is to live in justice and righteousness. The prophet Micah, a contemporary of Isaiah, was similarly concerned for justice. It is this prophet who in chapter 6 of his book summarises the demands of God: we are called to "do justice, love fidelity and go humbly with God".

Jeremiah and his contemporaries

I have become a laughing-stock all the day;
everyone derides me.

(Jeremiah 20:7)

Towards the end of the seventh century another great
prophet comes on the scene. Jeremiah will be involved in
the events of the final decades of the kingdom. He will
foresee and live through the destruction of Jerusalem.
As he begins his prophetic career a minor prophet by the
name of Zephaniah is also preaching. He reprimands the
people for worship of false gods and social injustice. His
strong words inspired the opening of the Christian hymn
Dies irae (Day of Wrath), which was used in the ancient
Latin form of the Funeral Mass. The young Jeremiah is
similarly concerned about the religious and social situation
of his people. The call of Jeremiah in chapter 1 sees him
respond: "I do not know how to speak. I am only a boy."
In his early years Jeremiah must have lived through the
religious reforms of the young king Josiah which were an
attempt to remove foreign influences from worship. All
sacrifice was to take place in the temple of Jerusalem.

The domination of Assyria had lasted for more than one
hundred years when in 612 BC the Assyrian empire was
taken over by the Babylonians. Another minor prophet,
Nahum by name, rejoiced at the fall of the oppressive

Assyrian empire. But the kingdom of Judah soon had to submit to a new empire, the Babylonians, under king Nebuchadnezzar. Jeremiah interprets the heavy Babylonian yoke as a punishment for Judah's constant infidelities. He warns the king and the people that they should accept Babylonian domination as brought on them by God. Jeremiah is viewed as a traitor. Judah does not heed the prophet's words and stupidly revolts against Babylon. Nebuchadnezzar besieges Jerusalem, deports the king and his family, nobles and artisans to exile in Babylon. He removes the treasures of the temple and the royal palace and appoints Zedekiah, the king's uncle, to rule in Jerusalem. Another prophetic book, that of Habakkuk, expresses outrage at the cruelty of the Babylonians.

The nation is now torn in two, with the leaders in exile in Babylon and Zedekiah attempting to exert authority over those left in Jerusalem who are hungry for power. Jeremiah continues to advise submission to Nebuchadnezzar. The people must yield to Babylonian control. During this period the prophet Jeremiah is the victim of further ill-treatment. At one stage he is lowered into a cistern to sink into the mud. The book of Jeremiah contains some powerful poems of the prophet, known as the "confessions", in which he expresses his strong emotions about his fate as a prophet of the Lord.

Zedekiah is persuaded to rebel against Babylon by the ambitious new leaders. Jerusalem now enters its darkest hours. A Babylonian siege lasts for eighteen months. The book of Lamentations contains anguished poems bewailing the fate of the city. Famine during the siege gives way to slaughter, rape and destruction once Jerusalem falls. A second deportation to Babylon takes place. What has become of God's promises? Why has God abandoned Jerusalem? Jeremiah was quite clear that the people had brought such destruction on themselves.

Jeremiah does provide some words of hope. In chapter 31 the prophet speaks of a new covenant which God will establish with the people. God will write the law on their hearts. People will understand the law as life-giving. Jeremiah is taken to Egypt when the situation in Judah remains dangerous. It is presumed that he died there.

Ezekiel, second Isaiah and the remaining prophets

The Lord God says: I am going to seek out my flock myself and search for them.

(Ezekiel 34:11)

After destruction of the city of Jerusalem and two deportations our focus must move to the land of Babylon. The people have lost their land and their temple. They are in danger of losing their faith too. It is the prophet Ezekiel, a member of a priestly family who was deported with the king in the first deportation, who is the first to give the people hope in the land of Babylon. Before the destruction of the city the prophet warns those deported with him of the coming disaster. Despite this God has not abandoned them. In the first chapter of the book, Ezekiel has a vision of a chariot on which God is brought to Babylon. God comes to be with the people in their exile.

Once the news of the destruction of the city is received Ezekiel addresses the problem of a people who have lost all hope. He proclaims a new hope. The people should turn back to God, who will see their change of heart. With various speeches Ezekiel encourages hope and new faith in those who have lost everything. The prophet uses the image of the shepherd in chapter 34 to speak of the selfish and negligent rulers of the past. Now it is God who will shepherd the people, take them home and provide for all their needs. God will raise up a new David as their protector. The famous vision of the dry bones brought back to life in chapter 37 proclaims new hope amid despair. The spirit will bring new life. The final chapters of the book contain a lengthy and complex vision. Amid details of plans for the rebuilding of the temple there emerges in chapter 47 a beautiful picture of the waters flowing from the temple and transforming the wilderness by the power of God's presence. God who was with them in exile will live with the people once more in their own land.

An anonymous prophet continues this tradition of giving hope to those in Babylon. This is the prophet whose words are set down in the book of Isaiah from chapter 40 to chapter 55. This prophet is given the conventional name of Second Isaiah or Deutero-Isaiah. His poems are among the most beautiful in the entire Old Testament. His work begins with the words "Console, console my people." The whole message is one of comfort. The prophet speaks of a God who is both able and willing to save the people. He speaks of a God who is both creator of all and lord of history. This God will summon the Persian ruler Cyrus who will take over the Babylonian empire and allow deported peoples to return to their own lands. Cyrus is referred to as God's chosen one, God's anointed one. Cyrus will have Jerusalem and its temple rebuilt.

The later poems of Second Isaiah celebrate the beauty of the rebuilt city, personified as Sion, bride and mother of countless children. Those who return from the exile in Babylon are amazed at God's intervention to bring them home, and give them a new start. Despondency and hopelessness give way to rejoicing and optimism. Multitudes will return to live in the city. The desert will bloom, the population will increase, the spirit will be given and an everlasting covenant established. God will also call all the nations to the city. There is no other God and Israel is both a witness to God's goodness and a servant of God. Four major poems provide images of God's servant, a servant who brings justice, a servant who speaks for God, a servant who is persecuted, and a servant whose suffering

44

is a sacrifice for others. Christians have always seen these poems as fulfilled in Jesus.

After the return from exile at the command of Cyrus king of Persia other minor prophets emerge. The work of rebuilding is encouraged by the prophet Haggai. This prophet assures the people that God will bless them abundantly once the temple of God is rebuilt. The book of Zechariah is made up of two sections, the first dominated by visions of God, the second belonging to a later period. The final chapters of the book of Isaiah, from chapter 56 to chapter 66, also belong to the period after the return. Further poems of Sion are found here expressing great hope, but there are also speeches which betray disappointment, injustice and even violence. The prophet encourages social justice so that the light of the nation may shine for others.

Four more minor prophets remain to be mentioned. In the book of Obadiah, a short book of twenty-one verses, a prophet reprimands the neighbouring Edomites for taking advantage of Jerusalem's fall by occupying new territory. Malachi deals with specific problems of the resettled community. The prophet looks to the coming of the day of the Lord, and the sending of a messenger to prepare for that day. The book of Jonah is unique. It contains the extraordinary story of a prophet who is unwilling to preach conversion to the Assyrians. The book has the clear message that God's love reaches out to all nations.

Finally the book of Joel also speaks of the day of the Lord. He proclaims the gift of the spirit on all peoples. The prophets express the hopes of Israel, hopes which for Christians are fulfilled in the coming of Jesus. The Old Testament looks forward to the New, where its hopes and promises are realised.

The Psalms and the Wisdom Books

> Give thanks to the Lord for he is good, for his faithful
> love lasts for ever.

> *(Psalm 136:1)*

The book of Psalms is among the most treasured of all
the books of the Old Testament. For centuries the psalms
have provided inspiration for the prayer of both Jews
and Christians. For Christians they constitute a large
part of liturgical and private prayer. The genius of the
psalms is that they arise from a variety of human
situations as the prayers of individuals and groups. They
are animated by joy, thanksgiving and praise, by pain,
anger or fear, longing or despair. They voice emotions
across the centuries.

Trust in God amid the dangers of life is expressed in a
unique way in the psalm which begins "The Lord is my
shepherd." Numbered as Psalm 23 or Psalm 22 depending
on whether the tradition of the Hebrew Bible or Greek Bible
is being followed, this psalm exemplifies the potential of
these prayers which speak to people's hearts and become
vehicles of their own prayer. While this psalm expresses
trust, Psalm 22 (21) is an anguished cry at God's absence:

"My God, my God, why have you forsaken me?" Christians revere these words as the last words of Christ in the Gospels of Matthew and Mark. The psalmist uses vivid imagery to describe his plight: he is a worm, not a man, scorned by all, hemmed in by many bulls and by dogs. He feels his life is poured away. Such psalms often end in praise of God as the psalmist gives thanks for God's intervention. Those who pray the psalms have ever new discoveries to make as they engage with the emotions of the psalmist.

Some psalms are very ancient but most can be related to the time of the monarchy or to the exilic and post-exilic periods. The psalms have traditionally been attributed to king David, who is remembered as a harpist and as the one who planned the building of the temple, but they seem to have been collected over many centuries, the whole collection probably being completed about 200 BC. Psalms especially important for Christians are those which, like the messianic poems of Isaiah, speak of the coming king. Psalm 72 (71) gives a portrait of an ideal king who establishes peace and justice throughout the world. The final psalm in the whole of the Psalter is a great hymn of praise with the repeated cry of "hallelujah", meaning "Praise the Lord!"

While the Psalter is unique, there is a small collection of books which as a group are known as "wisdom literature". These books are neither historical nor prophetic. They consider the problems of life in practical and philosophical ways. The writers reflect on life with all its variety and all its problems. The book of Proverbs is a collection of traditional teaching, much of it attributed to king Solomon. Much of the book is composed of short pithy sayings from the traditional wisdom of Israel and its neighbours. The book also contains longer poems, some of them in praise of wisdom. The book of Proverbs respects cherished beliefs and traditional understandings. It has no doubt, for example, that when a person suffers the suffering is the result of sin. It is this traditional view that is questioned in the book of Job.

The book of Job is the finest book of the wisdom tradition and contains some of the most beautiful and difficult poetry in the Old Testament. The book begins with the story of Job's misfortune. He loses his possessions and his family. He is struck down with sores and ulcers. Job remains virtuous, but cannot understand why such suffering has come his way. Three consolers of Job reiterate the traditional idea that suffering is self-inflicted. Job's repeated answer is one of bewilderment and rejection of their view. He cannot understand why God has allowed such suffering to befall him, and appeals to God. Finally, God gives Job an answer in a mysterious vision. The ways of God are beyond human understanding. God has given the whole of creation a wonderful freedom, but suffering and evil are present too. Job acknowledges God's greatness and that his human mind cannot fathom God's ways.

The book of Ecclesiastes, also known as Qoheleth from its Hebrew title, is like the book of Job in that it does not hesitate to challenge accepted opinions. While Job challenged one crucial view about God and human beings, Ecclesiastes raises the question of the value of wisdom and the pointlessness of pursuing it. "Vanity of vanities, all is vanity!" claims the writer. It is futile to strive for wisdom, or for pleasure, or wealth. Life itself is undermined by the inevitability of death. The writer realises that it is impossible for human beings to understand the work of God. The human mind cannot encompass all God's truth. Believers and readers of Scripture must know that they are on a long journey of discovery. Whatever they do discover is matched by the unknowable in God.

At this point mention can also be made of the Song of Songs, another book which might be considered a surprise entry in the Old Testament. The theme of its poems is the love of a man and a woman. The book celebrates this love, underlining the longing experienced in the absence of the loved one and the delight when the absent one arrives. The Song has often been seen by both Jews and Christians as pointing beyond human love to the love of God for the people, or of Christ for the Church.

The Book of Daniel and the Latest Writings of the Old Testament

The God of heaven will set up a kingdom
which shall never be destroyed.

(Daniel 2:44)

The books of wisdom are rather difficult to date since there are virtually no references to historical events. The book of Daniel, however, gives clear signs of being completed in the second century BC. The conquests of Alexander the Great in the fourth century led to the continuing dominance of Greek culture in the whole region of the eastern Mediterranean. In the early years of the second century the Jewish people were ruled by kings of Greek culture from neighbouring Syria. One of these, the infamous Antiochus Epiphanes IV, began a persecution of the Jewish religion. Details of his rule and of the Jewish revolt against him are found in the books of Maccabees. The final outcome was the establishment of an independent Jewish nation until the Roman occupation in the first century BC.

The book of Daniel was completed around the time of the persecution of Antiochus. It contains traditional stories about Daniel and his friends who survived trials and persecution as exiles in Babylon, stories which have a new relevance during this new time of trial. The later chapters of the book contain what are known as apocalyptic visions. Such apocalypses are found both in the Old Testament and in the New and outside the biblical material. They contain visions which reveal the future, God's intervention against evil, the establishment of God's reign, and the life beyond death of the people of God. The fundamental point made in these complex visions is that of God's enduring care for the people beyond persecution and beyond death. Israel's questionings about life after death receive a clear answer in the book of Daniel and in the stories of the Maccabean martyrs. God has prepared a life for the people beyond their present life.

Like the book of Daniel, the book of Esther speaks of danger experienced by the Jewish people. A Jewish community living in Persia is described as under threat of extermination. The orphan Esther is chosen to be queen due to her beauty but conceals her Jewish identity on the advice of her guardian Mordecai. Esther manages to frustrate the plan of the king's adviser Haman to annihilate the Jews. Another book has Judith as its heroine. This book, not found in the Hebrew canon, is, like Esther, of questionable historical value. It speaks of the Jewish heroine Judith, whose very name means "Jewess", who tricks her way into the Assyrian camp and decapitates the general Holofernes. Judith is praised for her beauty and her fear of God. Through her courage and her cunning she, like Esther, becomes the saviour of her people.

A more tranquil and domestic story is found in the book of Tobit, another one of those called "deutero-canonicals" due to its absence from the Hebrew canon. Two stories are interwoven here, the healing of the blindness of the old man Tobit, and the safeguarding of Sarah in her marriage to Tobias, the son of Tobit. It is the heavenly visitor Raphael who brings healing to both. Raphael's name means "God heals". The names of Tobit and Tobias both suggest that "God is good". This delightful book has a clear and powerful message about God's providence and goodness amid life's troubles.

The book of Baruch is another late, deutero-canonical book. Attributed to Jeremiah's scribe, it is in fact a collection of diverse material, including a prayer for God's forgiveness and a poem in praise of wisdom as a gift of God.

The final two books to be considered can both be classified as wisdom books. While the book of Ecclesiasticus (also known as Sirach) is a translation from Hebrew, the book of the Wisdom of Solomon was written in the Greek language. Ecclesiasticus is a long book which collects various pieces of traditional wisdom teaching. The book itself tells us that the teaching was compiled by a man called Jesus, son of Sira, or Sirach. It was called "Ecclesiasticus", which we might translate the "church book", for the Church valued its practical moral teaching. The book of Wisdom is much shorter and though written many centuries after his rule is attributed to Solomon. It even has Solomon speak about wisdom. It proclaims the belief that the virtuous who die are in the hands of God. Death is not God's final word to the people. This book, produced by Jews in Egypt, parallels the clear statements about life after death produced by faithful Jews during the persecution of Antiochus. The book of Wisdom praises God's continuing care for human beings. From the first page to the last page of the Old Testament this is an underlying theme.

The Old Testament in the New

Jesus said: It is accomplished.

(John 19:30)

The Vatican Council document *Dei Verbum* teaches us to value the Old Testament for its intrinsic worth and as the record of the continuing discovery of God by the people of Israel. We also treasure it as the Holy Scriptures used by Jesus, which were reaching completion at that time. When we read the New Testament we constantly come across quotations from the Old Testament and allusions to it.

The writers of the New Testament set out to present Jesus as the Son of God and the expected Messiah. It is quite natural that in order to explain what Jesus did and said, and to reflect on what God was doing in the sending of the Son, they should have constant reference to the older Scriptures. Each New Testament writer will use the Scriptures in a different way. Matthew's Gospel begins with a genealogy to connect the life of Jesus with the history of his people. As this Gospel progresses, on various occasions, the evangelist introduces words from the Old Testament with a statement such as "all this happened in order to fulfil this text". Other evangelists are less explicit, but connections to the Old Testament are present on every page. It is sufficient to survey the marginal references found in many Bibles to be aware of this. Every inspired writer has a way of utilising the Scriptures in order to explain Jesus and the new challenge of Christian faith. The writer of the Letter to the Hebrews, whose work is peppered with quotations from the Old Testament, remarks: "The word of God is alive and active, sharper than any double-edged sword." (*Heb* 4:12) This writer, like so many other Christians, wonders at the enduring power of the Scriptures of Judaism.

The New Testament uses the Old Testament to present Jesus as the fulfilment of Old Testament hopes. To the various portrayals of the expected Messiah will be added texts such as those concerning the "servant of the Lord" from the second part of the book of Isaiah. These and other texts play their part in the redefining of the role of the Messiah which Jesus himself brings about.

The Fathers of the Church, those early theologians of the Christian faith, also used the Old Testament to reflect on Christ. Old Testament figures such as Joshua and Jeremiah were seen to prefigure Jesus. They considered them "types" of Christ, figures who in some way prepare believers for the Messiah. Through the centuries Christians have reflected on the Old Testament in order to see new depths in the person of Christ. We might say that to deepen our faith every disciple of Jesus is called to make the journey through the Old Testament and into the New. Each believer's journey of faith is nourished and strengthened by the journey of the whole people of God, in the two testaments.

Church Teaching on the Bible

The Dogmatic Constitution on Divine Revelation, *Dei Verbum*, remains for us today the fundamental teaching of the Catholic Church on the Bible. Produced at the final session of the Second Vatican Council, it considers the nature of God's revelation to us in the Scriptures and in the Tradition of the Church. The revelation reaches its climax in Christ, who is described as the "fulness of revelation". *Dei Verbum* contains chapters on the inspiration and interpretation of the Bible, on the Old Testament, on the New Testament, and on Sacred Scripture in the Life of the Church.

Forty years after the end of the Council the Bishops of England and Wales, and of Scotland, produced a teaching document, based on *Dei Verbum*, entitled The Gift of Scripture. This is a user-friendly unpacking of the teaching of the Council, and also provides brief introductions to the different parts of the Bible. It remains highly relevant and useful today.

The most significant document on the Bible to emerge from the Catholic Church since *Dei Verbum* is the synod document entitled *Verbum Domini* (the Word of the Lord). After the introduction there are three principal parts:

'the Word of God', 'the Word in the Church' and 'the Word to the World'. The document looks back to *Dei Verbum*, which it describes as a milestone in the Church's history. It builds on the revival of interest in the Bible brought about by the Council.

In the first part, which considers 'the Word of God', Pope Benedict speaks of the word of God as the true light which all men and women need. Through God's word human beings can truly understand themselves and reach answers to their deepest questions. God's word offers "an openness to our problems, a response to our questions, a broadening of our values and the fulfilment of our aspirations".

In speaking of 'the Word in the Church' the document gives the most extensive coverage to the use of Scripture in the Church's worship. It is in the Church's liturgy that the voice of Christ is heard, speaking to the People of God. The Church is described as "the home of the word".

In the final part of the document, 'the Word to the World', the work of spreading the gospel is presented as the mission of all the baptised. It is directed not only to those who have never heard the gospel, but also to those societies where Christian faith has been lost and marginalised. Understanding and love of the Bible are essential to the new evangelisation.

A study guide, entitled 'The Word of the Lord: Discovering *Verbum Domini*', is also available to make the synod document more accessible. It is ideal both for private reading, and also for group sessions. The original document is summarised and accompanied by short extracts from the text itself. Those who use the study guide are invited to see it as a spring-board for tackling the original document with greater ease. There is a positive feast here of rich material for those who wish to engage more deeply with the Bible, and to become more familiar with Catholic teaching on the Scriptures.

Further reading on the Old Testament

The Dogmatic Constitution on Divine Revelation (Second Vatican Council) *Dei Verbum* (DO725) available from CTS. You can also view other titles from CTS at our website: www.ctsbooks.org

The Interpretation of the Bible in The Church, (Pontifical Biblical Commission), Pauline Books and Media. www.pauline.org

A. Graffy, *Alive and Active. The Old Testament Beyond 2000*, Dublin, Columba Press, 1999

L. Boadt, *Reading the Old Testament. An Introduction*, New York, Paulist Press, 1984

A. Ceresko, *Introduction to the Old Testament. A Liberation Perspective,* London, Chapman, 1992

H. Jagersma, *A History of Israel to Bar Kochba*, London, SCM Press, 1994

R. E. Murphy, *Responses to 101 Questions on the Biblical Torah*, New York, Paulist Press, 1996

R. E. Murphy, *Responses to 101 Questions on the Psalms and Other Writings*, New York, Paulist Press, 1994

Word of the Lord

Catholic Bishops' Conference of England and Wales

The recent Synod of Bishops in Rome which reflected 'The Word of God in the Life and Mission of the Church' was a grace-filled occasion to consider progress made since the Council and action to be taken in the years ahead.

This study guide to the Synod document, Verbum Domini, takes you through each section, offering explanations, activities and reflections.

Not just for Catholics, this guide is for anyone interested in how the understanding of the Bible develops.

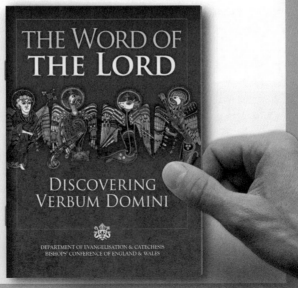

THE WORD OF
THE LORD

DISCOVERING
VERBUM DOMINI

DEPARTMENT OF EVANGELISATION & CATECHESIS
BISHOPS' CONFERENCE OF ENGLAND & WALES

Do871 ISBN 978 1 86082 851 5

The Gift of Scripture

Catholic Bishops' Conference of England and Wales

Fifty years ago the Second Vatican Council promulgated documents which still continue to guide the Church.

One of the greatest of these was the Dogmatic Constitution on Divine Revelation, popularly known as Dei Verbum. The Bishops of England and Wales, and of Scotland, in their teaching document The Gift of Scripture, build on Dei Verbum and subsequent Church teaching. This teaching document will further the 'new season of greater love for Sacred Scripture' promoted by Pope Benedict XVI in the Synod document Verbum Domini.

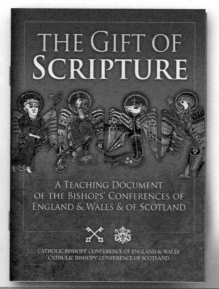

SC112   ISBN 978 1 86082 850 8

Discovering the New Testament

Fr Adrian Graffy

Pope Francis urges Christians to be nourished by the Word of God. Fr Graffy introduces all the books of the New Testament, giving advice for both private and liturgical reading of the Gospels, letters and other books. It is ideal for anyone wishing to understand and gain more from the New Testament, whether from their own personal reading, or listening to the readings at Mass. It is a companion to Fr Graffy's sister booklet 'Discovering the Old Testament'.

SC114 ISBN 978 1 86082 930 7